ROYCROFT
ART METAL

Kevin McConnell

1469 Morstein Road, West Chester, PA 19380

Combination pen tray/triple inkwell, 7" long, 4½" wide, and 2¾" high. Glass inkwell inserts are unsigned Steuben crystal. Late mark.
Original Price: Unknown.
Current Value: $275.00-$350.00.

Title page photo:
Radially hammered inkwell, 2¼" high and 3½" diameter. Contains the original glass liner. Late mark.
Original Price: $3.50 (circa 1928).
Current Value: $80.00-$110.00.

Published by Schiffer Publishing, Ltd.
1469 Morstein Road
West Chester, Pennsylania 19380
Please write for a free catalog
This book may be purchased from the publisher.
Please include $2.00 postage.
Try your bookstore first.

Copyright © 1990 by Kevin McConnell.
Library of Congress Catalog Number: 89-63420.

Printed in the United States of America.
ISBN: 0-88740-217-8

Contents

These bookends are among the most sought after Roycroft items owing to the strong design and superlative workmanship involved. 5½" high, 5¾" wide, highly embossed and detailed poppies framed by ornamental rivet-work. Note the subtle coloration of the poppies; this enameling was advertised in old Roycroft catalogues as "Italian polychrome". Early mark.
Original Price: $4.50 (circa 1910).
Current Value: $250.00-$350.00+.

Acknowledgements

This is the most important page in the book, for the simple reason that there wouldn't be any book without the help of the following people.

I am indebted to all of them for sharing their collections and knowledge, their sage advice, and especially for their friendship.

In no particular order, I extend my warmest thanks to: Marilyn Danielson, Vera Parry, Patrick Rankin, Mr. & Mrs. C.H.McConnell (AKA Mom & Dad), David Spillyards, Beverly Searcy, Seymour & Violet Altman, Robert Wyman Newton, Robert L. Gordon, Chester & Onda Dylewski, Williston Auctions, Bruce K. Beebe, Matthew & Beverly Robb, and Fire House Antiques.

A pair of bookends constructed from heavy, wrought strips of copper which are riveted to broad basal supports. 5¼" high. Middle mark.
Original Price:$6.00 per pair (circa 1910).
Current Value: $150.00-$200.00 per pair.

Introduction

Confessions of a Roycroft Collector

I first became aware of Roycroft art metal a few years ago, and what began as a casual interest in such items has metamorphosed into a full-scale obsession. That lone pair of Roycroft candlesticks that I started out with so long ago now has plenty of company—to the tune of well over a hundred pieces.

And there's no end in sight, which is a delightful aspect of the stuff. Regardless of how many pieces of Roycroft copper you have, there's always something else turning up to pique your interest and stimulate your greed center.

Which inevitably brings us to the why and the wherefore of this book. Having spent great chunks of time (and money) buying, collecting, and studying

Pair of 5½" long candlesticks, constructed of curled, hammered-copper with brass wash. Late mark.
Original Price: $6.00 per pair (circa 1925).
Current Value: $115.00-$140.00 per pair.

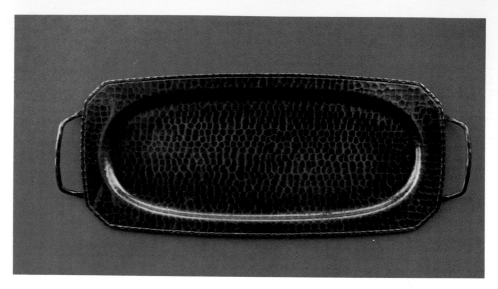

15" long cream and sugar tray. Exceptional hammering and dark brown patina. Middle mark.
Original price: $7.00 (circa 1915).
Current Value: $100.00-$140.00.

Roycroft metalware, writing and photographing a book on the subject certainly seemed to be a logical next step.

The purposes of this book are many fold, but especially to try to establish a coherent price scheme. With the hundreds of photos that appear in this book, I've made an effort to showcase a representative cross-section of the things that were made in the Roycroft Copper Shop, running the gamut from the most common to the most rare.

This book is by no means all-inclusive, and I'm not sure that any could be since such a vast quantity of Roycroft metal was made, some of which is unique or extremely rare.

Nevertheless, it is hoped that this publication will be of help and interest to Roycroft collectors everywhere, as it will offer some degree of insight into what was produced and what it is currently worth.

Because Roycroft copper was made for a period of about three decades, it is by far the most available, popular, and affordable of the Arts and Crafts metalware.

Collect it and enjoy.

Chapter One
Origins of the
Arts and Crafts Movement

A lot was going on in the world during the last decade of the 19th century, but in the midst of it all, a quiet revolution was taking place in both England and America which has come to be known as the Arts and Crafts movement.

In order to fully understand and appreciate Roycroft art metal, it is imperative to briefly discuss the philosophy behind the movement that spawned it.

In England, the Arts and Crafts movement had a number of proponents—John Ruskin, Thomas Carlyle, and particularly William Morris. Morris, a social reformer and leading spokesman for the movement strongly felt that the Industrial Revolution was detrimental, resulting in squalid working conditions as well as mass-produced goods of sub-standard quality and design.

Out of this milieu was adopted the medieval concept of Arts and Crafts guilds and communities, the purpose of which was to elevate the level of the

Two tier letter rack with a strong Arts & Crafts design on the front, decorative tracery, and folded over tip, 4¾" high. Early mark.
Original Price: $3.50 (circa 1910).
Current Value: $105.00-$130.00.

THE ROYCROFT SHOP

A portion of the Roycroft Community as it was pictured in the May 24 issue of *Roycroft*.

6″ diameter card tray with broad planishing marks and Arts & Crafts style design/work. Late mark.
Original Price: $1.50 (circa 1918).
Current Value: $75.00-$110.00.

Front and back views of a 3½" high match holder with nested ashtrays. Hammered-copper with rivetted construction and fine design work, including a pleasing Arts & Crafts motif and stippled edges on the match holder. Middle mark.
Original Price: $3.50 (circa 1915).
Current Value: $75.00—$95.00

worker to that of an artist by allowing the individual to hand-make items of simple beauty, virtue, and function. Among the things made were furniture, ceramics, books, wallpaper, fabrics, and of course, metalwork.

On the whole, the Arts and Crafts movement enjoyed its greatest popularity during the period of 1890-1910. And while the movement had its beginnings in England, the philosophy was eventually adopted and exploited in America by the likes of Gustav Stickley, Charles Limbert, and Elbert Hubbard.

1915 proved to be a devastating year for the American Arts and Crafts industry in that Stickley's firm, which produced Mission furniture and other accessories, went bankrupt, and Elbert Hubbard the guiding light of the Roycrofters perished aboard the *Lusitania*.

The movement limped along, but was never quite the same as changing tastes and competition in the form of the eschewed mechanization and mass-production finally brought the era to a close.

But, because they were so well made, Arts and Crafts objects have survived and abound for us to collect today, especially Roycroft art metal. By and large, we purchase these things for the same reasons that people originally did—beauty, function, and a high degree of craftsmanship.

Shouldered vase exhibiting a classic Arts & Crafts design. 5½" high, brass plating over hammered-copper. Photo of base reveals the prominent middle period Roycroft mark.
Original Price: $6.00 (circa 1915).
Current Value: $275.00-$350.00.

5¼" high vase, classic Arts & Crafts form. Early mark. Original Price: $6.00 (circa 1910). Current Value: $225.00-$275.00.

Chapter Two
Elbert Hubbard and the Roycrofters

It is impossible to discuss any sort of Roycroft collectible without first saying a few words about the man who was behind it all.

Elbert Hubbard, the founder of the Roycroft Community was many things in his day. Born in Bloomington, Illinois in 1856, he went to work as a salesman for the Larkin Soap Company at the age of 16.

Although he and his brother-in-law John Larkin went on to establish the financially successful J.D. Larkin & Co., Hubbard was not satisfied with his life and during the 1892/1893 period sold out his interests in the company and enrolled at Harvard.

A non-conformist by nature, Hubbard quickly discovered that Harvard was not the place for him and he dropped out. From there, he set out on a walking

Oval, hammered-copper serving tray with highly decorative linework and designs, attached handles, 22" long. Early mark. Original Price: $10.00 (circa 1910). Current Value: $250.00-$300.00.

This classic portrayal of Elbert Hubbard by Roycroft artist Otto Schneider appeared on and in numerous Roycroft publications.

Three-light candelabra, 10¾" long and 4¼" wide. Sockets and attached bobeches riveted to undulating base consisting of four curled feet. Late mark.
Original Price: $6.00 (circa 1925).
Current Value: $110.00-$145.00.

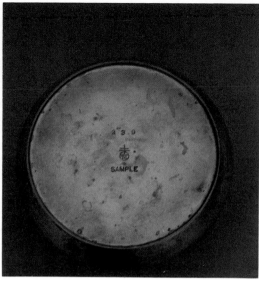

A very unusual 4½" high gourd-form vase with a 5¾" wide, oblate body and a short neck with an everted lip. Adding to the oddity of this piece are the base markings which include not only the early orb mark and production number 239, but the word "SAMPLE". This designation suggests that this item served as either a salesman's sample or perhaps even a reference example in the Copper Shop.
Original Price: $7.50 (circa 1910).
Current Value: $325.00-$375+.

tour of England, where he briefly met William Morris and had an opportunity to view the workings of the Arts and Crafts-oriented Kelmscott Press.

Greatly enamored of literature, Hubbard had written a novel entitled *The Man* which had been published under a pseudonym in 1891. Inspired by Morris and the Kelmscott Press, Hubbard returned to New York where he began to write again in earnest, this time a series of biographical sketches called *Little Journeys*.

Unable to find a publisher for them, he finally resolved to print them himself. Following Morris's lead, he established the Royscroft Press in East Aurora, located twelve miles south of Buffalo, New York.

Both books and periodicals soon flowed from Hubbard's prolific pen gaining him much fame and

Hammered-copper vase, wide mouth and bulbous form. 4¾" high. Late mark. Original Price: Unknown. Current Value: $165.00-190.00.

fortune. He, in turn, used his success to establish the Roycroft Community. Founded and operated on Arts and Crafts ideals, The Roycroft Community was nonetheless a business enterprise which at its peak production in 1910 employed over 500 workers for the purposes of furniture-making, book-binding, weaving, and metal-smithing.

Besides being a nationally famous author, publisher, editor, philosopher, and lecturer, Hubbard also possessed the charismatic ability to attract many gifted craftsmen to the Roycroft Community. Among then were: Karl Kipp (Copper Shop master craftsman), Dard Hunter (designer), and Louis H, Kinder (master bookbinder).

By 1915, Hubbard's community and his career were a fabulous success. He was writing, editing and publishing a variety of Roycroft periodicals such as *The Philistine*, and had authored literally dozens of books and essays including *A Message to Garcia*, an inspirational piece with a printing estimated at forty million copies.

But tragedy struck on May 7, 1915 when Elbert Hubbard died on the ill-fated *Lusitania*. And so a stunned Roycroft Community lost its leader and the first chapter came to an untimely end.

Leadership of the Roycroft facilities and business was quickly assumed by Hubbard's son, Elbert Hubbard II or Bert as he preferred to be called. Bert did not presume to be his father, but he was bright, shrewd, and kind—and that was enough.

His first business decision was a brilliant one, which involved a system by which Roycroft books, copper, and leather items were sold to department and gift stores throughout the country. This had multiple repercussions since these items had previously been available to the public only through the mail or by visiting the campus itself.

What resulted were increased sales and productivity, plus a greater variety and distribution of Roycroft objects (especially metalware). This is important for today's collectors.

In all likelihood, it was this new distribution policy that helped to stabilize the Roycroft Community and keep it in business long after the Depression had ravaged other business enterprises.

However, the aftermath of the Stock Market crash lingered on and eventually caught up with the Roycrofters. Sales slowed, craftsmen were let go, and in 1938 the Roycroft Community shut down.

Bert Hubbard had fought the good fight, keeping his father's dream alive for another 23 years—often operating under difficult circumstances and insurmountable odds.

He did everything he possibly could and is affectionately remembered for having done so.

Roycroft dome-form paperweight, 2" high, 3" diameter. Hammered-copper with an attached finial, which is fitted over a cast iron, lead-filled framework. No mark. Original Price: Unknown. Current Value: $40.00-$60.00.

Miniature hammered-copper bookends, made specifically for small edition books such as the one shown, which the Roycrofters also made. From left to right: 3¼" high bookends with stylized floral motif, brass finish over hammered-copper (middle mark); 3½" high bookends with Art Nouveau floral design and folded-over top (middle mark); 3" high triangular bookends with chipped edges (early mark).
Original price: $2.00 per pair (circa 1910-1915)
Current Value: $60.00-$70.00 per pair.

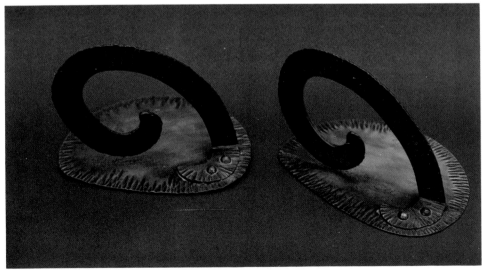

Abstract bookends with broad, radial hammering and large riveted construction. 4" high, brass wash. Late mark.
Original Price: $10.00 per pair (circa 1925).
Current Value: $140.00-$190.00 per pair.

Chapter Three
Karl Kipp and the Roycroft Copper Shop

The origin of Roycroft hand-wrought art metal can be traced back to the turn of the century. During this time, Elbert Hubbard was in the process of expanding the Roycroft campus, which meant the construction of several new buildings including the famous Roycroft Inn.

When it came for the finishing touches, Hubbard naturally chose to hire local craftsmen to hand-fashion such items as door hinges, andirons, lighting fixtures, and furniture hardware.

Quick to intuit a possible market for such hand-made metalware, Hubbard had the Roycroft Copper Shop built, staffed, and manufacturing wrought iron and copper items for purposes of sale by 1906. But these early efforts were crude and clumsy; the Copper Shop needed a talented catalyst to direct their efforts and that person was to be Karl Kipp.

This 4" high pewter vase is a representative example of the type of work that was done by Karl Kipp at his Tookay Shop. Note the elaborate maker's mark on the base, but be aware that items are sometimes simply marked with the double "K" symbol.
Original Price: Unknown.
Current Value: $150.00-$200.00.

THE COPPER SHOP

The Roycroft Copper Shop as it appeared on the cover of the November, 1929 issue of *The Roycrofter*.

Cylinder vase with applied nickel-silver decorative band. 6″ high, 3″ diameter, Karl Kipp design. Middle mark.
Original Price: $5.00 (1915).
Current Value: $600.00-$800.00+.

8½" high flower-holder, Karl Kipp design. Rivetted construction with glass tube insert, copper base and handle exhibit fine vertical and horizontal hammered texturing. Early mark.
Original Price: $2.00 (circa 1910).
Current Value: $95.00-$135.00.

In his own special way, Karl Kipp was as talented and interesting as Elbert Hubbard. At the age of 27, this balding ex-banker arrived on the Roycroft campus, yet another convert to Hubbard's charismatic call for individuals to come live and work in East Aurora.

Upon his arrival in 1908, Kipp was assigned to the Roycroft bookbindery. Sensing greater talents, however, Hubbard eventually placed him in charge of the fledgling Copper Shop where he and it were to flourish.

It would seem that with no prior training or experience, Kipp possessed an amazing and almost innate ability to fashion as well as to design copper and other metal items. Many of Kipp's designs are quite distinctive, having such qualities as riveted construction, nickel-silver overlays, and cut-out squares.

With his own great skill and Hubbard's encouragement, Kipp was able to make the Copper Shop prosper. By as early as 1909, Kipp had transformed the craftsmen into a talented, cohesive unit, allowing

Karl Kipp designed bud vase. Pyramidal base with rivet-attached handle and glass crystal insert, 8½" high. Prominent Textured hammering technique evident overall. Early mark. Original Price: $2.00 (circa 1910).
Current Value: $95.00-$135.00.

the Roycrofters to release a catalog featuring a great variety of hand-wrought metalwares that were available for sale that year.

In almost no time at all, Karl Kipp had not only assumed the position of Master-Craftsman, but also had put the Roycroft Copper Shop on the right track. On the whole, the Copper Shop continued to run smoothly in 1910 and 1911 as new designs were added and business boomed.

In 1911 though, Kipp and his eminently talented assistant Walter U. Jennings quit the Roycroft Copper Shop to form their own business, the Tookay Shop also located in East Aurora.

During the 1911 to 1915 period, Kipp and Jennings made wrought copper, pewter, and silver items, many of which bear a striking resemblance to Roycroft art metal of the same era. Tookay Shop metalwork is a highly collectible Roycroft-related item which is identifiable by an impressed mark consisting of the initials KK (the first one being reversed) enclosed within an orb.

Pair of Karl Kipp designed candlesticks, 8″ high. Square sha
prominently riveted to a four sided, pyramidal base, deep can
socket with attached bobeche. Closely-spaced vertical a
horizontal hammering technique evident on overall candlestic
Early mark.
Original Price: $4.00 per pair (circa 1910).
Current Value: $400.00-$550.00 per pair.

In spite of the roughly four year long absence o
Kipp and Jennings, the Roycroft Copper Shop
continued to thrive; an inarguable testament to
Kipp's organizational abilities. During this time, there
is evidence to suggest that Kipp, Jennings, and their
Tookay Shop endeavor were doing quite well. They
even maintained a New York City sales and display
room for their wares.

Unfortunately for everyone involved, fate had
other plans--namely World War I. On May 7, 1915
Elbert and Alice Hubbard were among those to lose
their lives when the *S.S. Lusitania* was torpedoed and
sunk by a German submarine off the coast of Ireland

In the aftermath of this great tragedy, Elbert
Hubbard II took over his late father's position at th
Roycroft campus. Among his first duties was t
request that Kipp and Jennings return to the Roycrof
Copper Shop, which they did in 1915.

Shortly after their return, Elbert Hubbard
implemented a new sales and distribution polic

which resulted in greatly increased production in the Copper Shop. Kipp was kept busy and happy coming up with constant new designs which were made in turn by the staff of about thirty-five craftsmen.

And so it went until the Stock Market Crash of 1929. As the Depression set in, Roycroft sales began to steadily decline and employees were gradually let go. Probably seeing the inevitable writing on the wall, Karl Kipp retired from the Copper Shop in the early 1930s, and the Roycroft campus finally and reluctantly closed its doors in 1938.

Set of four pin-on blotter corners. Hammered-copper high-lighted with conventionalized florals and linework. Note that only one of the four corners bears the Roycroft mark, which is typically the case. Middle mark.
Original Price: $4.00 (circa 1914).
Current Value: $80.00-$110.00.

Chapter Four
The Roycroft
Symbol and Marks

Most examples of Roycroft art metal bear their distinctive impressed shop mark consisting of a stylized cross below which is the letter "R" within an orb. As one might imagine, this symbol was not randomly chosen but is in fact full of meaning and messages.

The basic mark itself is patterned after one which was utilized by Cassiodorus, the medieval French monk and illuminator. Elbert Hubbard saw the symbol as being comprised of three basic parts, which he intended to represent Faith, Hope, and Love. The letter "R" stands, of course, for Roycroft which is variously thought to have been derived from *roi craft* meaning Royal Craftsman or King's Craft, as well as from the name of the English printers Thomas and Samuel Roycroft.

Semi-circular and arch-form bookends, 3½"-4" high. Early mark (left) and middle mark (center and right).
Original Price: $2.00 per pair (circa 1910-1915).
Current Value:$55.00-$75.00 per pair.

In any case, it is the mark which collectors look for, since it is likewise a symbol of great quality and value. Over the years, the Roycrofters marked their hand-wrought copper wares with variations of this symbol which can be used to approximately date them as described below....

Early Mark (circa 1906-1910)
Distinguishing Features: Both the head and tail of the letter "R" are tightly looped or curled.

Middle Mark (circa 1910-1915)
Distinguishing Features: Both the head and the tail of the letter "R" are approximately straight.

Late Mark (circa 1915-1938)
Distinguishing Feature: The word "ROYCROFT" is added below the orb mark.

ROYCROFT

Contemporary Mark (currently in use)
Distinguishing Feature: Double R's, the first one being reversed, the combination of which stands for "Roycroft Renaissance".

While the vast majority of Roycroft metalwork bears one of the above marks, it is important to be aware that unmarked pieces *do* exist. There are a variety of reasons why such items went unsigned, but mainly because in their spare time, the Copper Shop craftsmen made objects for their own personal use which were rarely stamped since they were not intended to be sold.

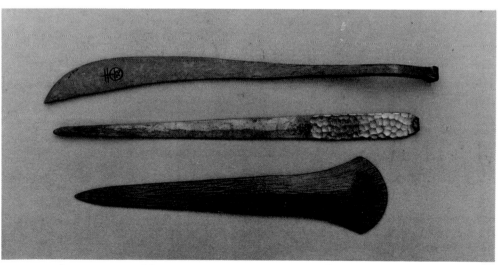

A grouping of letter openers. From top to bottom: a broadly hammered letter opener made from a thick gauge of copper (early mark); a letter opener exhibiting both coarse and fine hammering techniques, with a folded-over handle tip (middle mark); a radially-hammered letter opener with dark brown patina (middle mark).
Original Prices: .75, .50, and $1.40 respectively, (circa 1910-1915).
Current Values: $35.00-65.00 each.

Likewise, apprentice-made items which were not of sufficient quality were rejected without marking. The point is that unmarked pieces surface from time to time and that they can be positively identified as being Roycroft in origin through the use of old Copper Shop advertisements and catalogues.

It would behoove the interested collector to acquire and study such ads, since the ability to recognize unmarked Roycroft art metal can often result in some fine bargains. While unsigned examples are not as valuable as their marked counterparts, they are still very much worth having, particularly if the price is right.

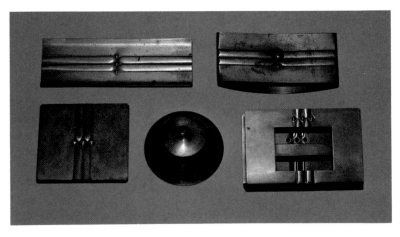

Roycroft five piece spun copper desk set consisting of: a pen tray, a rocker blotter, a stamp box, an inkwell, and a letter rack/calendar holder. All are decorated with an embossed line and diamond pattern. Late mark.
Original Price: $22.00 for the set (circa 1925).
Current Value: $150.00-$190.00 for the set.

Chapter Five
Pricing Roycroft Art Metal

A Few Words to the Wise

Along with most of the photographs of Roycroft metalware that appear in this book, an attempt has been made to research and quote the original prices of the items. And one thing that quickly becomes apparent is that when one considers the period during which it was made and the wages at the time, most Roycroft items were not particularly inexpensive.

For example, in 1925 not everyone was rushing out and buying a Roycroft lamp for $45.00 or a pair of "Big Six" candlesticks for $20.00. Quite simply, Roycroft metal items were at the time of their making considered high quality handmade objects of art that were accordingly priced for middle and upper-income families.

11½" high Roycroft table lamp, made from Steuben blue Aurene glass fitted with Roycroft acid-etched, silver-plated accouterments. Late mark.
Original Price: Unknown.
Current Value: $700.00-$850.00+

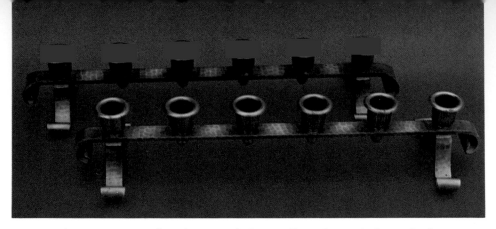

A massive pair of 16" long six-light candlesticks made from thick, precisely hammered strips of brass-plated copper which have been formed and riveted together. Referred to in original Roycroft catalogues as the "Big Six", this style of candlestick was likewise made in three-light ("Trindle") and eight-light ("Straight Eight") variations. Middle mark.
Original Price: $20.00 per pair (circa 1915).
Current Value: $350.00-$475.00 per pair.

Consequently, Roycroft art metal, which was so highly considered and priced during its heyday, has continued to increase in value as more and more collectors seek it out. Within the last few years, Arts and Crafts objects have become the darlings of the collecting public and this awareness has caused prices to rise sharply, Roycroft copper items included.

As the Arts and Crafts mania rages on, with no apparent evidence of subsiding, there exists a pricing problem for Roycroft art metal in the form of uneven values. For example, a 6" high, Karl Kipp designed Roycroft cylinder vase with applied nickel-silver band has sold for as much as $1500.00, yet current price guides reflect a $200.00-$300.00 price range.

The problem is obvious. What I've tried to do in the pages that follow is establish and present what I feel to be are honest, middle-range values. For instance, the vase mentioned above has been priced at $600.00-$800.00 which I contend is a lot closer to the truth.

In closing, I'd like to remind collectors that I'm not saying they should or have to pay the prices set forth in this book, I am instead stating that the objects are worth a certain amount, but if you can buy them for less then you're getting very good value and being a smart shopper.

Chapter Six
Evaluating Roycroft Metalware

For a wide variety of reasons all of which will be discussed, not all Roycroft art metal was created equal and thus prices are going to vary accordingly. When a collector considers a Roycroft purchase, they would do well to evaluate it as follows.

Condition: If the piece is bent or dented or if the patina is worn or compromised in some manner, then the item is simply not as desirable or valuable and should be priced accordingly.

Workmanship: While most Roycroft copper items reflect a high level of workmanship, not all of them do. Objects vary according to the skills of the individual craftsman who made them, some of whom were apprentices. One should not pay a lot for these secondary examples.

A pair of heavy, hammered-copper bookends with decorative rivets and attached rings. 5¼" high. Early mark.
Original Price: $6.00 (circa 1910).
Current Value: $150.00-$200.00 per pair.

No. 0118. Hand-wrought Copper Paper Knife, 50 cents

No. 0120. Hand-wrought Copper Pin Tray
Size, 4 x 6½ inches; $2.00

Although crude and unwieldy, these two Roycroft items dating from 1906 were the first attempts at copperwork and are therefore much sought after by collectors.

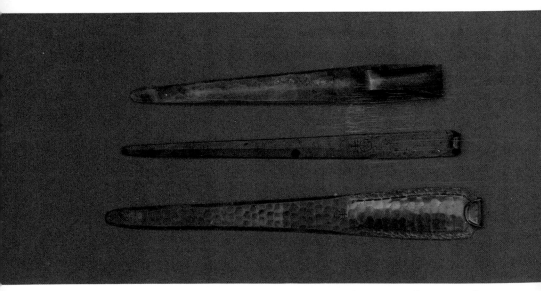

An assortment of three letter openers of varying design and workmanship. From top to bottom: 8" long with middle mark, 8½" long with early mark, 9½" long with middle mark.
Original Price: .50 to $1.25 each (circa 1910-1915).
Current Value: $45.00-$65.00 each.

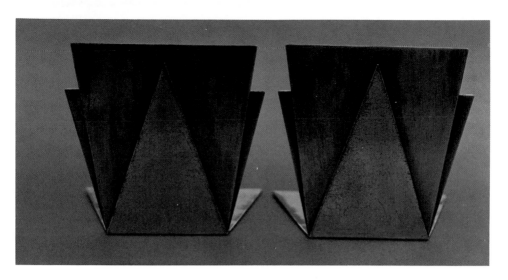

Pair of 5″ high copper bookends with triangular brass onlays.
Late mark.
Original Prices: $7.50 per pair.
Current Value: $95.00-$135.00 per pair.

Also entering into this area of discussion is the fact that Roycroft hammered-copper objects are of greater collector interest and value than the thinner gauge, smooth-formed items made by the copper-spinning process, because of the painstaking workmanship involved. While the latter are certainly collectible, they're not as expensive or as in demand as the hand-wrought pieces are.

Form: With the literally hundreds of different items that were made in the Roycroft Copper Shop over the years, it is obvious that some are going to be far more common and affordable than others.

In general, Roycroft items that were costly when they were originally made probably were not produced in the prodigious quantities that simple, inexpensive objects were. Because of this, Roycroft metalware such as ashtrays, letter openers, and many of the bookends are available and affordable, while complicated things like lamps, large candlesticks, and Karl Kipp designed objects are fast becoming very expensive.

The would-be collector should consider all of these factors before investing his or her money.

Unhammered 7½" long letter opener. Curvi-linear shape with bent-over top. Late mark.
Original Price: .60 (circa 1925).
Current Value: $28.00-$40.00.

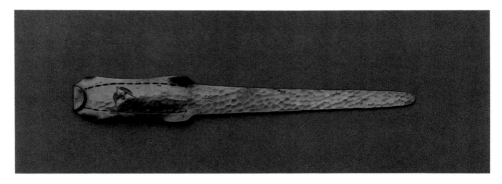

Finely hammered 9½" long letter opener with decorative crimping and trifoliate design. Middle mark.
Original Price: $2.00 (circa 1915).
Current Value: $50.00-$70.00.

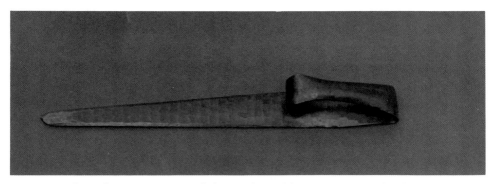

8" long letter opener exhibiting broad hammering and a folded over handle. Middle mark.
Original Price: $1.25 (circa 1915).
Current Value: $65.00-$85.00.

Chapter Seven

A Description of
Roycroft Surfaces

Yet another value factor that must be addressed as regards Roycroft art metal is the surface of the item, or to be more specific, the manner in which the piece was made. These include three basic methods that are described as follows.

Hand-Hammered: The most desirable and valuable of the Roycroft art metal items are those which were hand-hammered and made from heavy gauge copper. Although hand-hammered items were made throughout the duration of Copper Shop production (1906-1938), collectors are particularly interested in those pieces made prior to 1915, since most exhibit superior designs and workmanship.

Smooth-Formed: In an effort to reduce costs and to augment productivity, a thinner gauge of copper was used by the Roycroft Copper Shop during the 1920s. Also during the 20s and especially on into the 1930s, Roycroft art metal began to be produced by the

These three Roycroft items exhibit the different methods of manufacture, which from left to right include: smooth-formed, acid-etched, and hand-hammered.

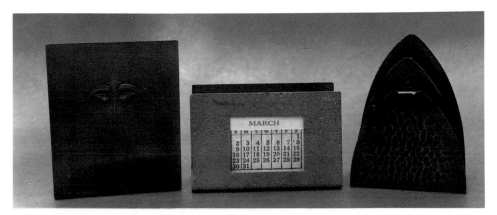

copper-spinning process. These smooth-formed items involved little or no hand-workmanship. Because of their plain appearance, such pieces are sometimes referred to as "blanks" and are not especially popular with collectors.

Acid-Etched: Also during the 1920s and the 1930s, many of the items made at the Roycroft Copper Shop by the copper-spinning process were given a decorative surface texture by immersing them in an acid solution. In effect, this acid-etching/texturing simulated the appearance of hand-workmanship. These pieces are moderately popular with today's collectors.

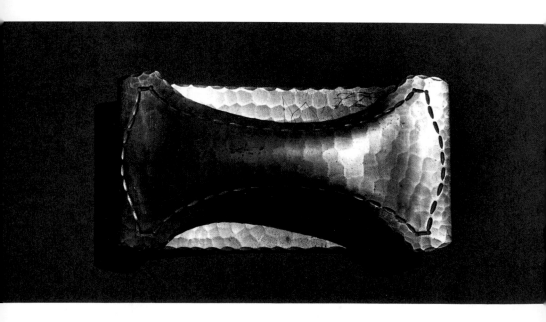

5" long rocker blotter, brass finish over hammered-copper. Decorative "stitched" linework and chipped edges. Middle mark. Original Price: $1.70 (circa 1915).
Current Value: $45.00-$65.00

Chapter Eight
Roycroft Patinas
The Finishing Touch

Collectors should be aware of the fact that the Roycroft Copper Shop made use of three basic finishes on their wares. Among these finishes are: **Aurora Brown** which is a dark chocolate brown patina that was achieved by exposing the copper items to ammonia fumes for a specific period of time; **Old Brass** which involved the brass-plating of the finished copper objects; and **Modern Sheffield**—a sterling or, sometimes, nickel-silver wash over copper.

Other patinas were experimented with, including a blue-green bronze-like finish which is rarely encountered. Probably the favorite finish with today's collectors is Aurora Brown, followed closely by Old Brass, and with Modern Sheffield being the least desirable. This is ironic considering that items with

Representative examples of the various patinas employed by the Roycroft Copper Shop, including: Old Brass, Aurora Brown, and Modern Sheffield.

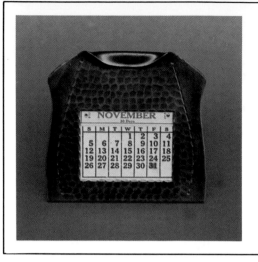

4" high perpetual calendar with crimped top and dark brown patina. Middle mark. Original price: $1.50 (circa 1915).
Current Value: $40.00-$65.00.

this finish were originally considerably more expensive than the brown or the brass.

However, with the current popularity of Arts and Crafts items in general and Roycroft art metal in particular, collectors are snapping up examples regardless of the finish. And more and more of them are discovering that owning Roycroft items in a variety of colors and patinas makes their collection even more attractive and interesting.

When considering the purchase of a Roycroft copper item, an essential factor is not just the patina, but, more importantly, the *condition* of the patina. That is to say, if the patina is heavily worn, has been removed through polishing, or has been recently restored through the use of acids , then the object in question is far less desirable and valuable than a comparable item in mint condition.

All in all, the Roycroft collectors best investment are those wrought copper items with original, mint patina. Of course, there's nothing wrong with purchasing worn, polished, or repatinated pieces (especially the hard-to-find ones) as long as they're fairly priced.

Polished copper items that have been repatinated have been immersed in commercially available acid solutions and are usually recognizable as such by a splotchy and uneven reddish-brown finish as opposed to the original Roycroft patina which is smooth and consistent.

Chapter Nine
Roycroft Art Metal
Rarity Chart

Although all Roycroft copper items are very collectible, some are considerably more available than others. It is hoped that the following breakdown of items will help to quickly familiarize you with what is common and what is rare, and allow you to choose your purchases accordingly. It is generally safe to assume that you will see common items for sale time and again, but the rarer things tend to come onto the market rather infrequently and, if at all possible, should be purchased when they do.

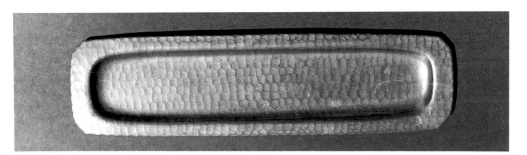

9½" long pen tray, brass wash over hammered-copper. Late mark.
Original Price: $2.00 (circa 1925)
Current Value: $35.00-$50.00.

Group One/Very Common: most ashtrays, letter openers, and other single desk items, bookends of simple design, and matchbox holders.

Group Two/Common: small bowls and vases, simple candlesticks, crumb trays, desk sets, card trays, vasettes, many of the bookends, smooth-formed items, most sconces and ivy hangers, nut plates and bowls.

20" high table gas lamp made from a combination of wood, slag glass, and copper. 8¼" square oak base supports copper uprights and large slag glass panel shade. Note the diamond-shaped hammered-copper tag affixed to the base which bears the early orb mark.
Original Price: Unknown.
Current Value: $2000.00-$2500.00+.

Group Three/Relatively Rare: large serving trays, unusual bookends, large bowls and vases, Kipp designed bud vases and candlesticks, complex desk items such as large pen blocks, as well as double and triple inkwells, elaborate sconces and ivy hangers, picture frames, cigar and cigarette boxes, and complete smoker's sets.

Group Four/Rare: lamps of all kinds, especially hanging lights with slag glass panels, large and complicated pairs of candelabra/candlesticks, Karl Kipp designed objects with nickel-silver overlays or cut-out squares, complete chafing dishes.

In addition to the above, there are also a number of Roycroft metal items which while not extremely valuable are nonetheless elusive. Such things would include: hat pins, door knockers, place card holders, book marks, jewelry, napkin rings, tea-bells, and newspaper holders.

Chapter Ten
Roycroft Renaissance
An Arts and Crafts Update

Long after the Roycroft Community fell silent, there remained a strong general interest in the Arts and Crafts movement and in Elbert Hubbard and the Roycrofters.

Largely because of the continued belief in such philosophies and ideals, the Roycroft Community lives again. Today, traditional Roycroft furniture and other items are being produced by craftsmen there, and are available for sale in the refurbished Copper Shop.

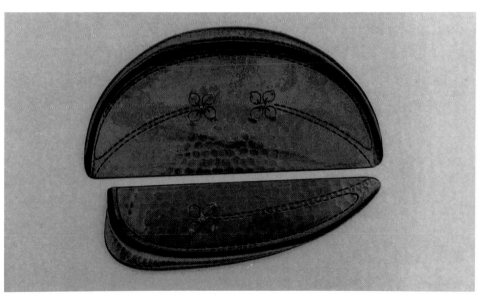

8½" X 4" crumb tray and matching 7¾" X 2½" scraper decorated with a stylized Dogwood flower design. Only the larger of the two pieces exhibits the Roycroft mark. Middle mark.
Original Price: $3.00 (circa 1915).
Current Value: $95.00-$135.00.

Each hand-made item is distinguished with a new yet familiar mark—the orb and cross, but incorporated within it are two R's, standing for "Roycroft Renaissance." All in all, the campus is a busy place once more, and so Elbert Hubbard's dream lives on.

The memory and accomplishments of Elbert Hubbard (left) and his son Bert (right) provide inspiration for the Roycroft Renaissance.

Crumb tray (6" X 4") and scraper (5½" X 3½"), dark hammered-copper with decorative protrusions simulating rivets. Of these two items, only the tray is marked with the Roycroft symbol. Middle mark.
Original Price: $2.50 (circa 1915).
Current Value: $85.00-$120.00.

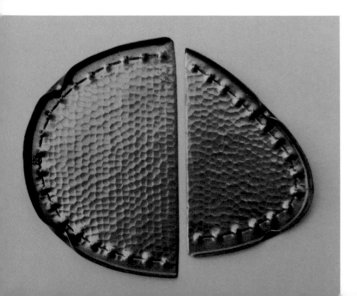

Chapter Eleven

Roycroft Art Metal Photo Descriptions

Bookends

4¾" high owl bookends. Riveted construction, stylized owl motif within octagonal, stippled reserve. Middle mark.
Original Price: $4.00 per pair (circa 1915).
Current Value: $130.00-$170.00 per pair.

5¼" high bookend with applied strap (exhibiting finely textured hammering), prominent rivets, and an attached ring. Middle mark.
Original Price: $5.00 per pair (circa 1915).
Current Value: $150.00-$200.00 per pair.

Three bookends of varying sizes, shapes, and workmanship displaying the same stylized floral design. The miniature bookend is 3½" high, while the larger ones are each 5¼" high. Middle mark (left and center), late mark (right).
Original Price: $2.00 per pair (small), $4.00 per pair (large).
Current Value: $60.00-$90.00 per pair.

A grouping of triangular form bookends. Large bookends are 5" high, the miniature one is 3" high. All bear the early mark.
Original Price: $2.00 per small pair, $2.50 per large pair (circa 1910).
Current Value: $60.00-$95.00 per pair.

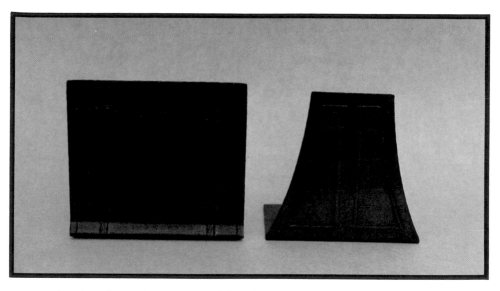

Bookends with geometrical floriforms, each is 4½" high. Middle mark.
Original Price: $3.50 per pair (circa 1915).
Current Value: $90.00-$120.00 per pair.

Bookends of differing designs and techniques, all are 5" high. Middle mark (left and right), late mark (center).
Original Price: $3.00-$4.50 per pair (circa 1915-1925).
Current Value: $65.00-$100.00 per pair.

Pair of bookends, 8½" high and 5¾" wide, one with a highly embossed flower, the other open to display fancy book covers such as the one which is shown. Early mark.
Original Price: Unknown.
Current Value: $160.00-$200.00 per pair.

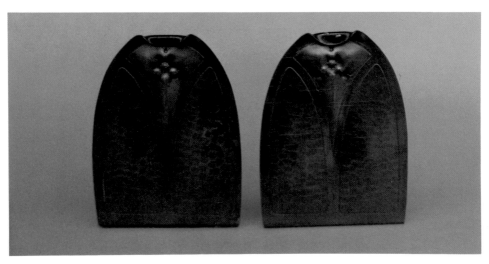

Arch-form bookends with dark brown patina and elongated trifoliate motif. 5" high. Middle mark.
Original Price: $3.00 per pair (circa 1915).
Current Value: $75.00-$95.00 per pair.

A pair of 8½" X 5¾" open-style bookends intended for displaying leather-bound volumes of books with ornate covers. Early mark.
Original Price: Unknown.
Current Value: $140.00 per pair.

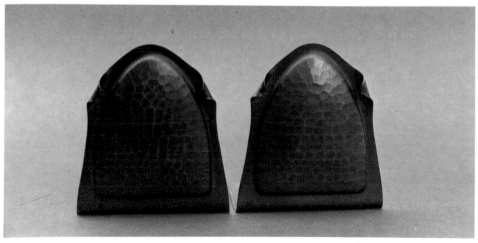

Arch-form bookends with relief-hammered panels and crimped edges, 4" high. Late Mark.
Original Price: $2.20 per pair (circa 1925).
Current Value: $65.00-$85.00 per pair.

5¼" high oval-form bookends with brass-plating and applied decorative wire work. Middle mark.
Original Price: $5.00 per pair (circa 1915).
Current Value: $85.00-$110.00 per pair.

Triangular bookends with crimped tips, rivet-attached bases, and semi-circular reserves depicting stylized potted plants and flowers. Middle mark.
Original Price: $4.00 per pair (circa 1915).
Current Value: $150.00-$200.00 per pair

3½" high triangular bookends with crimped tips and decorative traceries. Middle mark.
Original Price: $2.50 per pair (circa 1915).
Current Value: $75.00-$95.00 per pair.

4¼" high bookend with crimped top, brass wash, and stylized peacock design within a stippled reserve. Early mark.
Original Price: $4.00 per pair (circa 1915).
Current Value: $150.00-$200.00 per pair.

Arch-form bookends with decorative embossing and crimping, 4" high. Late mark.
Original Price: $2.50 (circa 1925).
Current Value: $65.00-$85.00.

A pair of heavy-gauge, hammered-copper bookends with vertical tooling, decorative crimping, and riveted construction. 5" high. Early mark.
Original Price: $3.50 per pair (circa 1910).
Current Value: $130.00-$160.00 per pair.

A pair of 3½" high arch-form bookends, slightly excuravate in form, with decorative notched edges. Middle mark.
Original Price: $2.50 (circa 1915).
Current Value: $75.00-$95.00.

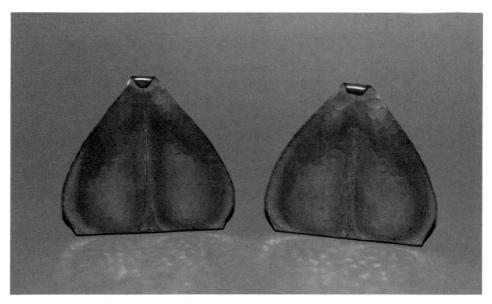

A pair of 4¼" high philodendron leaf design bookends. Early mark.
Original Price: $2.50 per pair (circa 1910).
Current Value: $100.00-$125.00.

Bowls and Trays

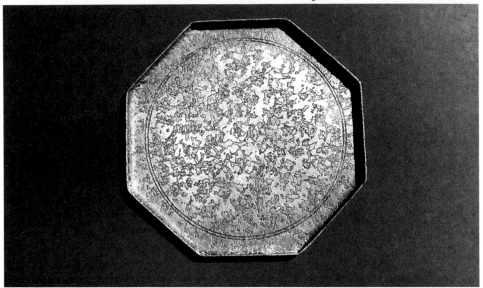

Octagonal card tray, 6¾" square. Acid-etched texturing with silver over copper finish. Early mark.
Original Price: $2.50 (circa 1910).
Current Value: $125.00-$160.00

Bowl with gently tapering shoulders and oblate body, 6" diameter. Middle mark.
Original Price: $4.00 (circa 1915).
Current Value: $130.00-$175.00

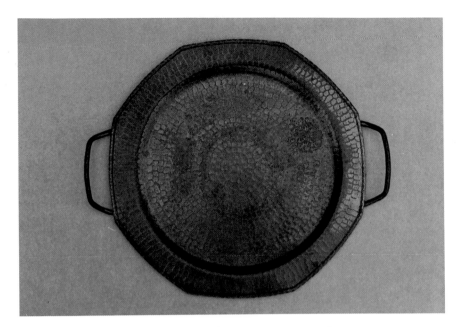

Octagonal serving tray, 10" diameter. Late mark.
Original Price: $5.50 (circa 1928).
Current Value: $140.00-$180.00.

Set of nut bowls with serving spoon; small bowls are 4¾"
diameter, master bowl is 8" diameter, spoon is 6½" long. All
items are interiorally hammered-copper with a matching
trifoliolate design. Early mark.
Original Price: $12.00 per set (circa 1910).
Current Value: $200.00-$250.00 per set.

Bowl, 4″ diameter, crimped rim design. Early mark.
Original Price: $2.50 (circa 1910).
Current Value: $75.00-$100.00.

Small bowl with squat, tapered body and decorative tooling below the lip. 2½″ high, 4″ basal diameter. Middle mark.
Original Price: $2.50 (circa 1915).
Current Value: $70.00-$90.00.

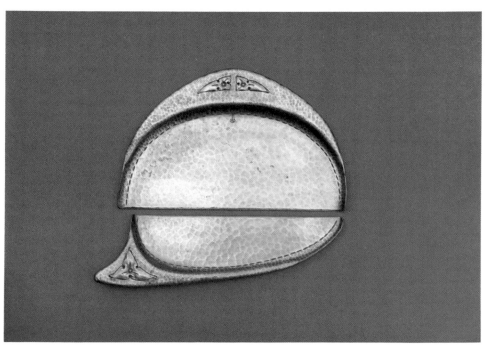

Matching crumb tray (8″ X 5″) and scraper (9″ X 3″) with brass wash and embossed trifoliate design. Early mark.
Original Price: $3.00 (circa 1915).
Current Value:$85.00-$120.00

Side and top views of an acid-etched compote with silver finish.
5″ high, 11″ diameter. Middle mark.
Original Price: $10.00 (circa 1915).
Current Value: $175.00-$225.00.

6" diameter card tray with crimped rim and decorative tooling.
Middle mark.
Original Price: $2.00 (circa 1915).
Current Value: $65.00-$85.00.

Round serving tray, 15½" in diameter, handles attached with
large rivets. Middle mark.
Original Price: $5.00 (circa 1915).
Current Value: $200.00-$250.00.

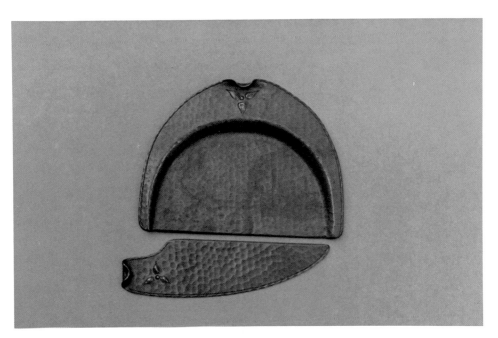

Crumb tray (7½" X 5½") and scraper (8" X 3"), finely hammered with decorative crimping and trifoliate designs. No mark.
Original Price: Unknown.
Current Value: $65.00-$85.00.

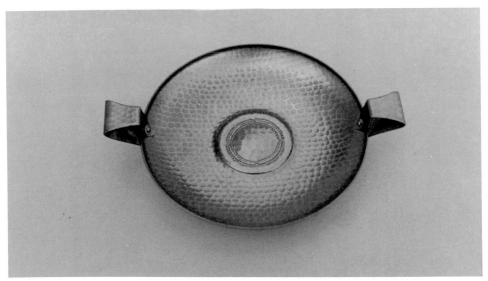

Hammered-copper card tray with graceful rivet-attached handles. Exceptional workmanship and patina. Overall diameter 9", height 1¾". Middle mark.
Original Price: $6.00 (circa 1915).
Current Value: $135.00-$175.00.

Large, 15″ diameter octagonal serving tray (shown with the smaller 10″ diameter version for contrast). Middle mark.
Original Price: Unknown.
Current Value: $175.00-$225.00.

Nut or fruit bowl, 9″ diameter, 3¼″ high. Finely hammered surface with detailed embossing and linework. Middle mark.
Original Price: $10.00 (circa 1915)
Current Value: $200.00-$250.00.

6″ diameter card tray with crimped corners, tooled interior edges, and stylized flowers. Middle mark.
Original Price: $2.50 (circa 1915).
Current Value: $100.00-$125.00.

Large round tray with attached handles, 18″ greatest diameter. Early mark.
Original Price: $5.00 (circa 1910).
Current Value: $225.00-$275.00.

Hammered-copper bowl with decorative tooling below the lip.
2¾" high, 7" diameter. Middle mark.
Original Price: $4.00 (circa 1915).
Current Value: $110.00-$140.00.

Small, hammered-copper bowl with rolled lip, tapered body, and broad, circular base. 4½" high, 5" diameter at top. Middle mark.
Original Price: $5.00 (circa 1915).
Current Value: $105.00-$130.00.

Unhammered-copper bowl with applied base and folded lip, 4"
high and 8½" in diameter. Late mark.
Original Price: Unknown.
Current value: $80.00-$105.00.

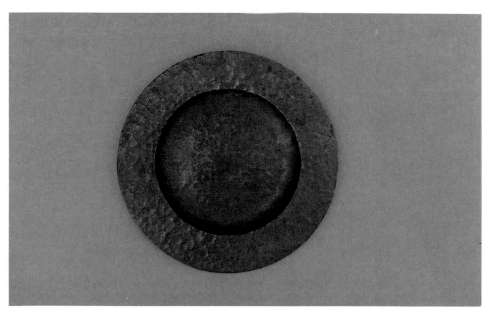

Hammered-copper pin tray, 4½" in diameter. Middle mark.
Original Price: $1.00 (circa 1915).
Current Value: $45.00-$65.00.

Hammered-copper bowl with worn silver finish and crimped, scalloped lip. 2½" high, 6" diameter. Late mark.
Original Price: $4.00 (circa 1925).
Current Value: $70.00-$100.00

Desk Items

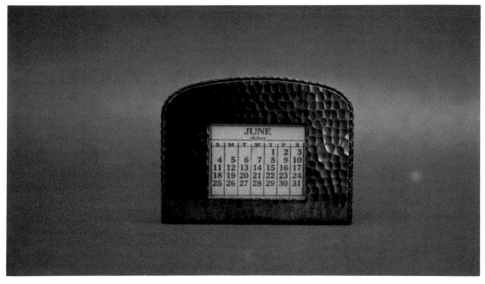

Perpetual calendar, 3½" high, 4½" long. Linework incised at edges, brass finish. Middle mark.
Original Price: $1.00 (circa 1915).
Current Value: $38.00-$55.00.

Perpetual calendar, 3¾" high, broad radial design-work at top.
Late mark.
Original Price: $1.50 (circa 1925).
Current Value: $60.00-$80.00.

Semi-circular stationary holder with bold radial hammering and
brass wash. 3" high and 5½" long. Late mark.
Original Price: $2.60 (circa 1928).
Current Value: $95.00-$125.00.

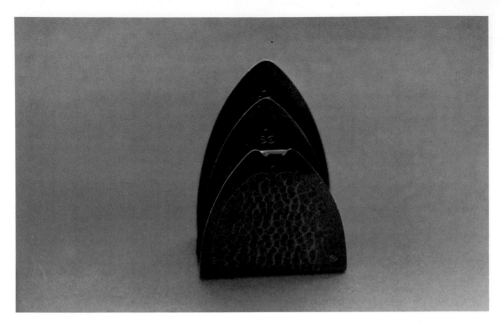

5″ high triangular stationary holder, hammered-copper with flowing, decorative linework and folded-over tip. Dark patina and rivetted construction. Middle mark.
Original price: $3.50 (circa 1915).
Current Value: $80.00-$100.00.

Perpetual calendar, 3½″ high, with brass wash and folded-over tip. Middle mark.
Original Price: $1.50 (circa 1915).
Current Value: $40.00-$60.00.

Perpetual calendar/stationary holder, 7½" long. Late mark.
Original Price: $7.50 (circa 1925).
Current Value: $140.00-$185.00.

Letter rack, 6" long and 4" high, linework at edges, hammered-
copper with dark brown patina. Middle mark.
Original Price: $3.00 (circa 1915).
Current Value: $90.00-$120.00.

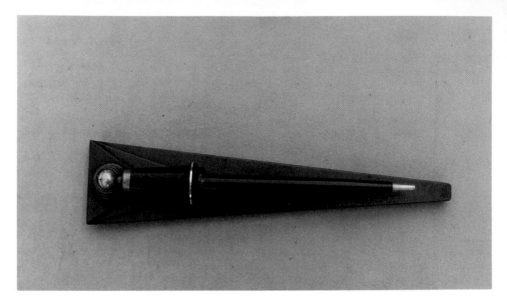

8½" long pen-holder. Base consists of a ⅛" thick piece of unhammered-copper over which additional triangular designs have been overlapped. Attached to this base is a brass and Bakelite Parker pen and holder. Late mark.
Original Price: $9.00 (circa 1925).
Current Value: $55.00-$70.00.

Inkwell, 2¾" square, 1¾" high. Stylized floral design on lid, inkwell contains the original glass insert. Early mark.
Original Price: $3.00 (circa 1910).
Current Value: $90.00-$115.00.

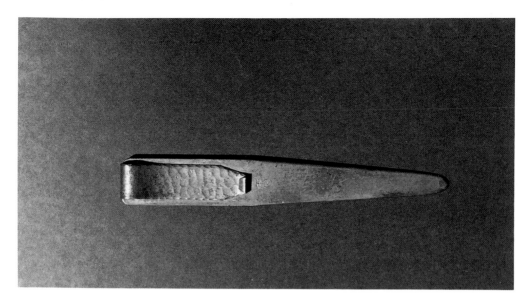

Brass-plated letter opener, 8″ long. Smooth blade with applied hammered-copper handle. Middle mark.
Original Price: $1.00 (circa 1915).
Current Value: $30.00-$45.00.

Finely hammered pen tray with an embossed floral motif. 9¾″ long, 3¼″ wide. No mark.
Original Price: Unknown.
Current Value: $35.00-$45.00.

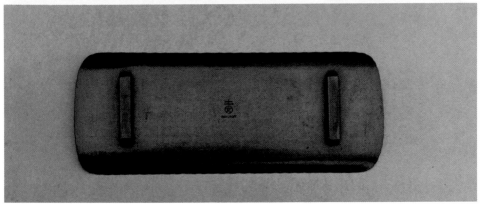

7" long pen tray, slightly curved in form, "stitched" linework frames the edges, attached rectangular feet on base. Late mark.
Original Price: $2.00 (circa 1919).
Current Value: $50.00-$65.00.

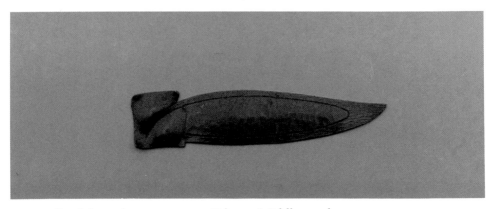

Leaf-form letter opener, 6" long. Middle mark.
Original Price: .75 (circa 1915).
Current Value: $45.00-$60.00.

Spun copper letter rack/calendar holder. 3¼" high, 5" long, 2¼" wide. Late mark.
Original Price: $2.60 (circa 1925).
Current Value: $35.00-$45.00.

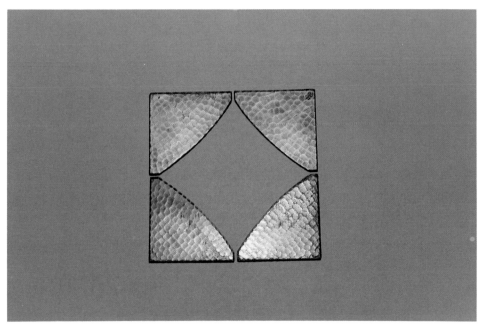

A set of four 3" X 3" slip-on blotter corners. Brass plating over hammered-copper. Middle mark.
Original Price: $5.00 (circa 1915).
Current Value: $75.00-$95.00.

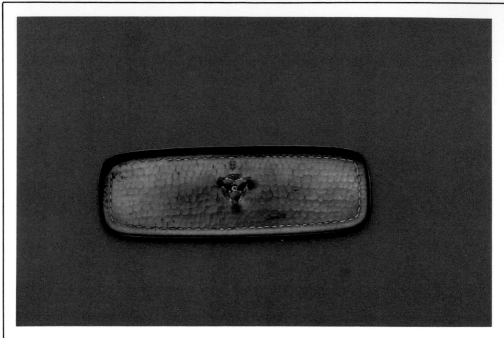

8¾" long pen tray with prominent trifoliate design in center and decorative linework framing the edges. Middle mark.
Original Price: $2.00 (circa 1915).
Current Value: $55.00-$70.00.

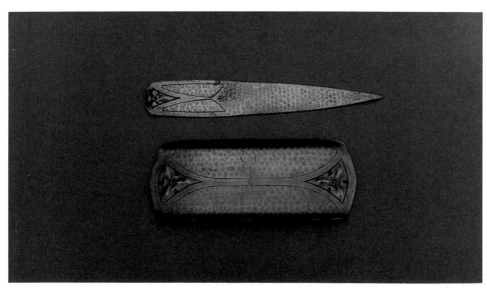

Matching pen tray (7" long, 3" wide) and letter opener (8¼" long), decorated with an elongated trifoliate design and incised linework. Middle mark.
Original Price: $4.00 for both (circa 1915).
Current Value: $90.00-$120.00 for the set.

3″ square Steuben glass inkwell with a Roycroft hammered-copper lid. Overall height is 3½″. Middle mark.
Original Price: $5.50 (circa 1915).
Current Value: $95.00-$135.00.

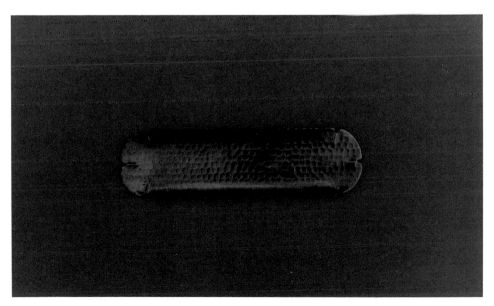

8″ long pen tray with incurvate form and scalloped ends. Middle mark.
Original Price: $2.00 (circa 1915).
Current Value: $55.00-$65.00.

3¼" high smooth-formed letter rack decorated with an embossed line and diamond design. Late mark.
Original Price: $2.60 (circa 1925).
Current Value: $70.00-$85.00.

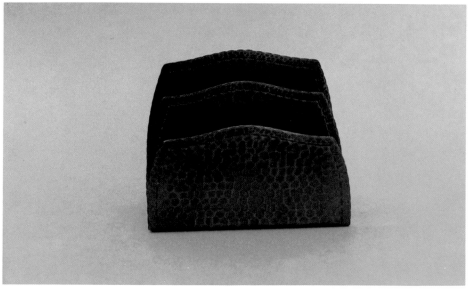

3½" high letter rack, exhibiting both fine and broad hammering techniques and a dark brown patina. Middle mark.
Original Price: $3.00 (circa 1915).
Current Value: $95.00-$125.00.

3″ high pen and pencil holder with bluish-green patina. Rectangular base measures 4″ long by 2″ wide. Middle mark. Original Price: .75 (circa 1915). Current Value: $50.00-$65.00.

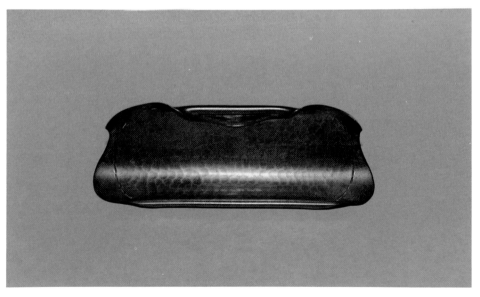

7¼″ long pen tray, curvilinear form with ornamental crimping. Middle mark. Original Price: $1.00 (circa 1915). Current Value: $50.00-$60.00.

Arch-form perpetual calendar exhibiting a dark brown patina and an embossed leaf/floral motif. Middle mark.
Original Price: $1.50 (circa 1915).
Current Value: $65.00-$85.00.

Finely hammered 2¾″ high inkwell with decorative linework and dark brown patina. Middle mark.
Original Price: $4.00 (circa 1915).
Current Value: $115.00-$140.00.

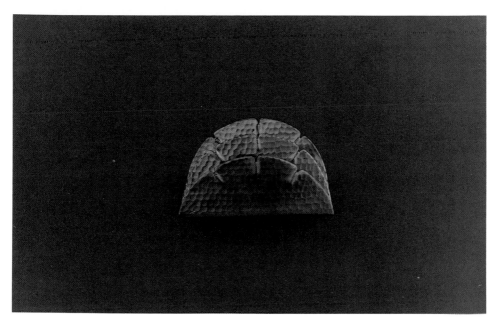

Two section arch-form letter rack with scalloped edges. 3½"
high, 5" wide. Middle mark.
Original Price: $3.50 (circa 1915).
Current Value: $90.00-$115.00.

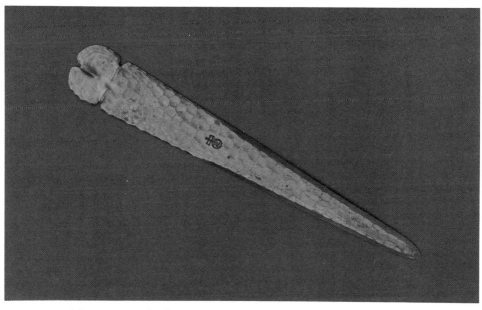

7¾" long triangle-form letter opener with beveled edges and
ornamental handle. Middle mark.
Original Price: $1.50 (circa 1915).
Current Value: $50.00-$60.00.

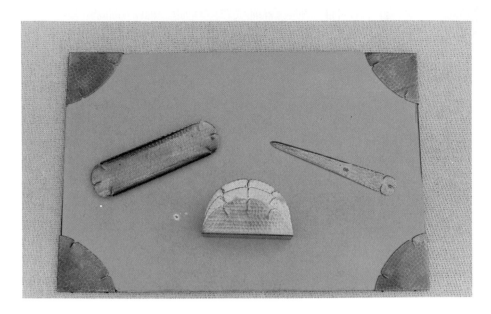

Roycroft hammered-copper desk set consisting of a pen tray, a letter opener, a letter rack, and a set of four blotter corners. Middle mark.
Original Price: $14.00 (circa 1915).
Current Value: $300.00-$350.00.

Slip-on blotter corners, 2½" X 2½", decorative radial hammering. Late mark. Original Price: $5.00 for set (circa 1925).
Current Value: $70.00-$90.00.

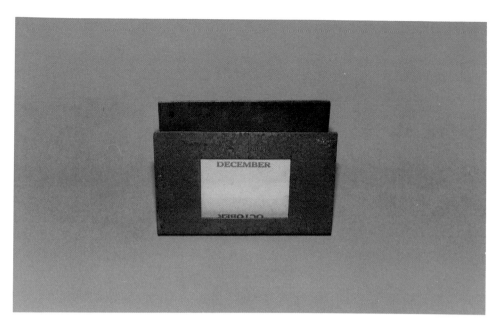

Letter holder/perpetual calendar, acid-etched with brass wash.
3¼" high, 5" long, 2" wide. Late mark.
Original Price: Unknown.
Current Value: $50.00-$70.00.

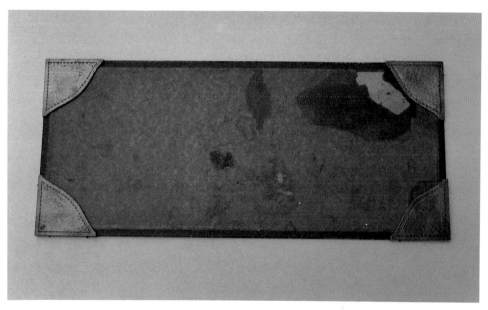

Set of four hammered-copper pin-on blotter corners with
original blotter. The corners are each 3½" X 3½". Middle mark.
Original Price: $4.00 (circa 1915).
Current Value: $90.00-$120.00.

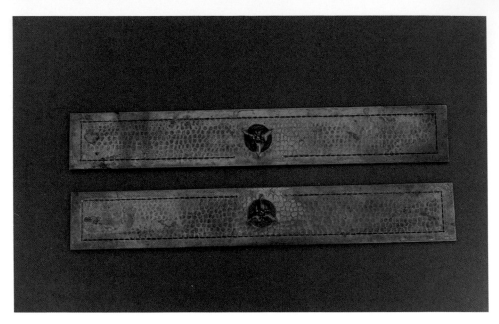

A pair of 16″ long blotter ends ornamented with stitched linework and a strong trifoliate design. Middle mark.
Original Price: $7.50 (circa 1915).
Current Value: $95.00-$135.00.

Radially hammered pen tray, 7″ long, 2½″ wide. Middle mark.
Original Price: $2.50 (circa 1915).
Current Value: $65.00-$80.00.

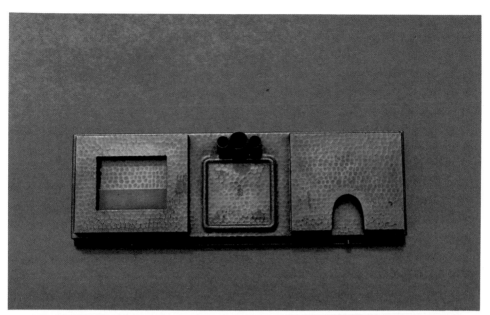

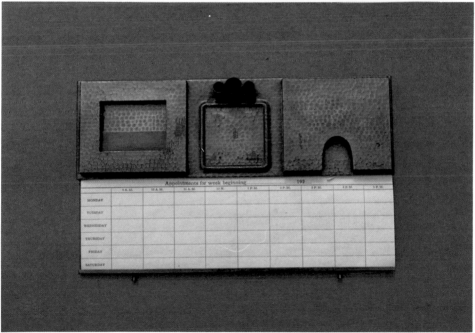

Originally sold as an "appointment set", this desk piece had space for a calendar (left), pens and pencils (top center), a note pad (right), and even had a pull-out drawer with an appointment pad. The square area in the center was intended for a glass inkwell. 2" high, 12" long, 4" wide. Middle mark.
Original Price: $15.00 (circa 1915).
Current Value: $350.00-$450.00.

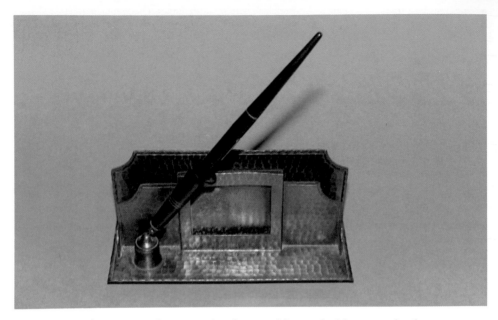

Combination ink pen, calendar, and letter holder, 3¼" high, 5" long, 2" wide. Late mark.
Original Price: $17.50 (circa 1925).
Current Value: $160.00-$195.00.

Exquisitely hammered inkwell with tapered body and dark brown patina, 2½" high. Late mark.
Original Price: $3.50 (circa 1925).
Current Value: $120.00-$150.00.

Smooth-formed pen tray, 7″ long, 2¼″ wide. Late mark.
Original Price: $2.00 (circa 1925).
Current Value: $30.00-$40.00.

Smooth-formed stamp box, 1″ high, 4½″ long, 4″ wide. Late mark.
Original Price: $3.50 (circa 1925).
Current Value: $40.00-$55.00.

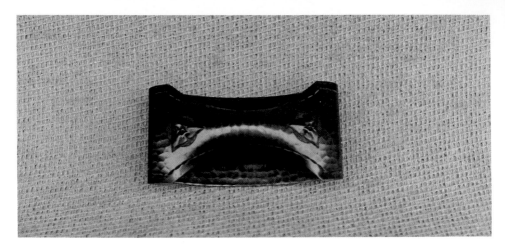

A 5″ long rocker blotter with dark chocolate brown patina and trifoliate designs embossed on the handle. Middle mark.
Original Price: $1.70 (circa 1915).
Current Value: $55.00-$75.00.

Lighting

A pair of unhammered 9¼″ high Art Deco style copper and brass candlesticks. Stacked disc base with decorative devices at top and bottom of shaft, flared bobeche attached to deep candle socket. Late mark.
Original Price: Unknown, these are possibly experimental pieces.
Current Value: $175.00-225.00 per pair.

Two arm reading lamp shown with and without shade. Made from a combination of heavy hammered and smooth-formed copper with a dark brown patina. Note the decorative wire work surrounding the base. 20" high. Middle mark.
Original Price: $45.00 (circa 1915).
Current Value: $1100.00-$1300.00.

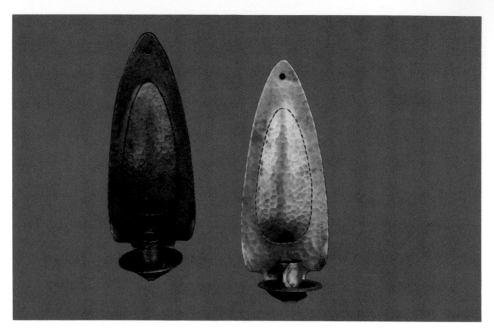

Pair of 8″ high wall-hanging sconces. Arrowhead-shaped back-plates with attached candle sockets. Early mark.
Original Price: $5.00 per pair (circa 1910).
Current Value: $150.00-$225.00 per pair.

2½″ high brass-plated candlestick with flared base, broad saucer, deep candle socket, and riveted handle. Middle mark.
Original Price: $2.25 (circa 1915).
Current Value: $80.00-$120.00.

Beautiful three-light candelabra measuring 20″ high. Flared saucer-form base supports the double twisted central shaft to which the two branches are attached. Middle mark.
Original Price: $12.50 (circa 1915).
Current Value: $550.00-$700.00.

Originally advertised as a "Mother Goose" candlestick, the top lifted off of this item thus allowing matches and spare candles to be stored in the bottom. 3" high, 6" diameter. Late mark.
Original Price: $5.00 (circa 1925).
Current Value: $120.00-$140.00.

18″ high Roycroft lamp with baluster-form body and leaded glass Art Deco shade. Base is 5″ in diameter, while the greatest diameter of the shade is 12½″. Acid-etched texturing. Late mark. Original Price: Unknown.
Current Value: $1800.00-$2000.00.

Roycroft's famous "Straight Eight" candlestick which measures a full 20" long. This example has an acid-etched finish and a brass wash. Height is 2¾". Middle mark.
Original Price: $12.50 (circa 1915).
Current Value: $325.00-$400.00.

Candlestick with broad saucer-form base, deep candle socket, and rivet-attached handle. 1¾" high, 5¼" diameter. Middle mark.
Original Price: $2.00 (circa 1915).
Current Value: $100.00 -$125.00.

A pair of spectacular 12½" high, twist-stem candlesticks with 5" diameter circular bases. Middle mark.
Original Price: $9.00 per pair (circa 1915).
Current Value: $600.00-$750.00 per pair.

Hammered-copper candlestick, 6½" high. Flared, sloping base supporting a tubular shaft to which is attached a wide, deep bobeche. Middle mark.
Original Price: $3.00 (circa 1915).
Current Value: $80.00-$100.00.

A pair of low candlesticks with crimped bases and brass plating. 2″ high. Middle mark.
Original Price: $4.00 per pair.
Current Value: $100.00-$135.00 per pair.

Candlestick with rivet-attached handle. 1¾″ high, 4½″ diameter. Early mark.
Original Price: $2.00 (circa 1910).
Current Value: $60.00-$75.00.

Roycroft hammered-copper electric lamp with helmet-form shade. Overall height is 13", the shade is 6½" in diameter. Middle mark.
Original Price: $10.00 (circa 1915).
Current Value: $1200.00-$1500.00.

14″ high Roycroft electric lamp with dome-form shade and 6″ square base. Early mark.
Original Price: $15.00 (circa 1910).
Current Value: $1500.00-$1800.00.

A pair of 8" high candlesticks with elegant floriform bases, finely hammered shafts topped by deep, widely rimmed sockets. Middle mark.
Original Price: $5.50 per pair (circa 1915).
Current Value: $225.00-$275.00.

A pair of 3½" high candlesticks with broad, round bases. Support columns are highlighted by circular decorative devices surmounted by candle sockets. Middle mark.
Original Price: $7.50 per pair (circa 1915).
Current Value: $110.00-$150.00 per pair.

Smoking Accessories

4" diameter octagonal ashtray with highly embossed diamond motif in center and attached cigarette rest. Middle mark.
Original Price: $1.75 (circa 1915).
Current Value: $40.00-$55.00.

Large 8¼" diameter ashtray with acid-etched surface and three attached cigarette rests. Late mark.
Original Price: Unknown.
Current Value: $60.00-$75.00.

4″ diameter circular ashtray with attached cigarette rest and mirror brass finish. Late mark.
Original Price: $1.00 (circa 1925).
Current Value: $30.00-$45.00.

Smooth-formed matchbox holders, 2¼″ long. Late mark.
Original Price: $1.25 each (circa 1925).
Current Value: $18.00-$25.00 each.

5¼" square matchbox and ashtray holder. Hammered-copper
with dark brown patina. 2¼" high. Middle mark.
Original Price: $5.00 (circa 1915).
Current Value: $80.00-$100.00.

Hammered-copper ashtray of graceful design, 2" high, 8"
greatest diameter. Late mark.
Original Price: $5.00 (circa 1926).
Current Value: $85.00-$110.00.

Nesting ashtrays, 4" diameter, trifoliate design in center. Middle
mark.
Original Price: $3.00 (circa 1915).
Current Value: $35.00-$50.00 for the set.

Ashtray with attached cigarette rest, 4½" diameter, 1" high.
Middle mark.
Original Price: $2.00 (circa 1915).
Current Value: $35.00-$50.00.

3½" high matchbox holder decorated with a stylized floral design. Late mark.
Original Price: $2.50 (circa 1925).
Current Value: $65.00-$85.00

Ashtray with attached cigarette rests, 5¼" diameter. Broad central planishing marks surrounded by coarse radial hammering. Smooth exterior with brass wash. Late mark.
Original Price: $2.50 (circa 1925).
Current Value: $60.00-$80.00.

Matchbox holder/ashtray, 3¾" diameter, 2¼" high. Top lifts off to access a nest of ashtrays. Middle mark.
Original Price:$4.00 (circa 1915).
Current Value: $75.00-$95.00.

Nested set of ashtrays, overall diameter 3¾″. Middle mark.
Original Price: $1.00 (circa 1915).
Current Value: $30.00-$45.00

Combination humidor/pipe-rack made from spun copper. 7″
high, 8″ basal diameter. Late mark.
Original Price: Unknown.
Current Value: $125.00-$160.00.

4" diameter ashtray, acid-etched with brass wash. Late mark.
Original Price: $1.00 (circa 1925).
Current Value: $25.00-$35.00.

Combination matchbox holder and ashtray caddie. Hexagonal 6"
diameter base accommodates six triangular ashtrays which lift
out. Central matchbox holder bears ornamental tooling and
crimping. Attached handle swivels and is radially hammered.
Overall height is 6". No mark.
Original Price: Unknown.
Current Value: $150.00-$175.00.

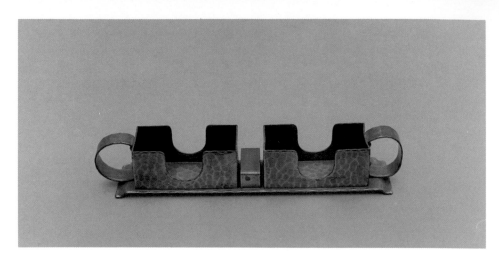

This particular smoking accessory was designed to hold two packages of cigarettes as well as a box of matches which fit into the central opening. 1½" high, 1½" wide, 9" long. Middle mark. Original Price: $5.00 (circa 1915).
Current Value: $80.00-$110.00.

Large ashtray of exceptional design and workmanship, 4½" high, 9¾" basal diameter. Heavy hammered-copper with brass details. Four attached cigarette rests, central shaft served as a pipe-knocker. Middle mark.
Original Price: $15.00 (circa 1915).
Current Value: $140.00-$175.00.

Ashtray with attached cigarette rest, 2½" square. Middle mark.
Original Price: $1.00 (circa 1915).
Current Value: $25.00-$35.00.

A grouping of 3" diameter silver-plated ashtrays, with interior
hammering and fluted edges. Late mark.
Original Price: .75 each (circa 1925).
Current Value: $22.00-$30.00 each.

Smooth-formed ashtray, 4″ diameter with dark reddish-brown
patina. Late mark.
Original Price: .50 (circa 1916).
Current Value: $20.00-$30.00.

4¼″ hammered-copper ashtray with stippled, chipped edges and
decorative linework. Early mark.
Original Price: $1.00 (circa 1910).
Current Value: $25.00-$35.00.

Beautifully made humidor, 8″ high and 5″ diameter. Cylindrical
form with ornamental wire work encircling the base. Matching
lid is slightly domed with an attached knob. Middle mark.
Original Price: $10.00 (circa 1915).
Current Value: $175.00-$225.00.

Vases

5½″ high copper vase with distinctive vertical hammering, ruffled rim, and brass finish. Late mark.
Original Price: $5.00 (circa 1930).
Current Value: $130.00-$180.00.

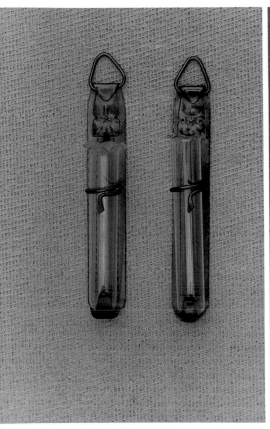

A pair of 10½″ long wall flower holders. Intricate floriform bases and relief-hammered trifoliate designs on the tops of the back-plates. Glass vial inserts with ruffled tops. Middle mark.
Original Price: $2.00 each (circa 1915).
Current Value: $80.00-$110.00 each.

4½″ high vasette consisting of a round, hammered base surmounted by three vertical leaf-life supports which hold a glass tube insert. Silver finish. Middle mark.
Original Price: .75 (circa 1915).
Current Value: $40.00-$65.00.

5¾" high vase with acid-etched finish. Late mark.
Original Price: $7.50 (circa 1918).
Current Value: $165.00-$200.00.

6" high Roycroft vase consisting of a hammered-copper floriform
base and a green Steuben Bubbly glass insert. Middle mark.
Original Price: $6.00 (circa 1915).
Current Value: $350.00-$450.00

6½″ high cylinder vase with reddish-brown patina and tooled decorative band highlighted with green enameling. Early mark.
Original Price: $7.50 (circa 1910).
Current Value: $275.00-$325.00.

Roycroft bud vase with a hammered-copper base and a fancy glass insert. Overall height: 4½″. Late mark.
Original Price: $1.60 (circa 1925).
Current Value: $60.00-$80.00.

8½" high baluster shape vase with ruffled floriform rim. Early
mark.
Original Price: $12.00 (circa 1910).
Current Value: $300.00-$375.00.

Hammered-copper bud vase, 6½" high. Vase consists of a thick, heavy disc base to which is attached a broadly hammered tube with a flared, crimped rim. Late mark.
Original Price: $2.00 (circa 1924).
Current Value: $65.00-$90.00.

10″ high cylinder vase with expanded base and flared mouth.
Acid-etched texturing with silver wash. Late mark.
Original Price: Unknown.
Current Value: $300.00-$425.00

A 7″ high cylinder vase displaying exquisite workmanship. Exceptionally fine overall hammering highlighted by a conventionalized vertical floral motif. Middle mark.
Original Price: $5.00 (circa 1915).
Current Value: $325.00-$400.00.

8¼″ high vase gently tapering body and brass finish. Early mark.
Original Price: $10.00 (circa 1910).
Current Value: $275.00-$350.00.

5″ high cylindrical vase with gently contracted base and mouth. Decorative tooled band highlighted with embossed, stylized flowers. Early mark.
Original Price: $4.75 (circa 1910).
Current Value: $160.00-$185.00.

Vertically-hammered 4½″ high vase with deep brown patina and gently closing top. Middle mark.
Original Price: Unknown.
Current Value: $120.00-$150.00.

Highly unusual "Etruscan" vase made from tooled copper finished with the rare blue-green patina. 8" high. Late mark. Original Price: Unknown. In all likelihood, this is an experimental design.
Current Value: $200.00-$250.00+.

5" high bud vase with 2¾" diameter circular base. Glass insert
fits into four vertical hammered-copper prongs. Late mark.
Original Price: $1.60 (circa 1925).
Current Value: $70.00-$95.00.

6" high bud vase with embossed 3" square flori-form base, attached wire handle, and glass tube insert. Middle mark.
Original Price: $2.00 (circa 1915).
Current Value: $90.00-$120.00.

Top, bottom, and side views of an unusual smooth-formed vase, measuring 5" high and 12" greatest diameter. Acid-etched surface and floriform handles. Late mark.
Original Price: Unknown.
Current Value: $350.00-$425.00.

Smooth-formed wall-hanging sconce, 8" long. Embossed oval design on backplate, candle socket and bobeche attached to base. Late mark.
Original Price: $3.50 (circa 1925).
Current Value: $45.00-$65.00.

Tea bell, 3½" high. Simple, elegant design with fine hammering and a brass wash. Middle mark.
Original Price: $2.00 (circa 1915).
Current Value: $55.00-$75.00.

Hammered-copper box with hinged lid which is slightly domed and has decorative linework. 1½" high, 5¼" long, 3" wide. Middle mark.
Original Price: $3.00 (circa 1915).
Current Value: $70.00-$90.00.

Potted plant holder. Dark, hammered-copper, 9½″ long. Middle mark.
Original Price: Unknown.
Current Value: $75.00-$95.00.

2″ high incense burner consisting of two curled feet supporting a
shallow, rimmed basin. Excellent workmanship and dark original
patina. Middle mark.
Original Price: $1.00 (circa 1915).
Current Value: $65.00-$85.00.

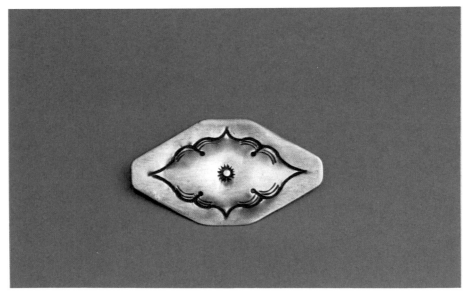

Roycroft sterling silver brooch measuring 2″ long and 1¼″ wide.
Reverse is marked with the words "ROYCROFT" and
"STERLING".
Original Price: $5.00 (circa 1930).
Current Value: $150.00-$185.00.

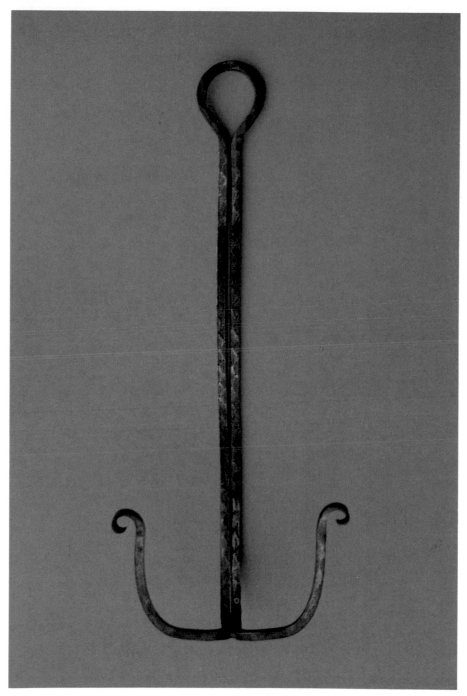

10" long ivy holder made from a single strip or hammered and bent copper. Middle mark.
Original Price: Unknown.
Current Value: $50.00-$70.00.

Ornate potted plant holder, 10¼" long, brass wash. Late mark.
Original Price: $6.00 (circa 1925).
Current Value: $80.00-$110.00.

Arch-form hammered-copper napkin ring made from a single strip of copper which was formed and riveted together. This particular example bears the initial "MJQ". 1" high, 3" long. Middle mark.
Original Price: $1.00 (circa 1915).
Current Value: $30.00-$45.00.

Hammered-copper kettle, 3" high, 4¼" diameter at top. Tripod legs and attached bail handle. Late mark.
Original Price: Unknown.
Current Value: $90.00-$120.00.

A very unusual and possibly unique Roycroft hammered-copper coffee pot, with an attached wooden handle and "Sheffield silver" finish. Overall height is 10", basal diameter is 4½", the spout is 5½" long, and the wooden handle is likewise 5½" long. Middle mark.

Original Price: Unknown, since this was probably a specially commissioned item rather than a production piece.

Current Value: Placing a value on this item is not possible at this time, since to the author's knowledge there is no precedent upon which to base it.

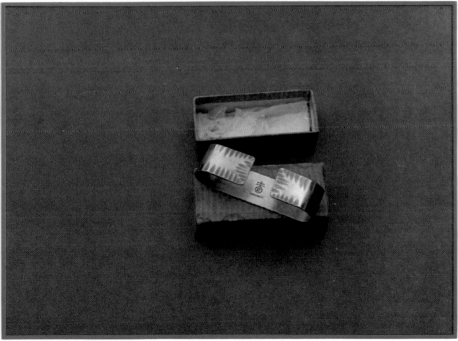

3″ long napkin ring shown with the original box. Broad radially hammered edges, and silver finish over copper. Late mark.
Original Price: $1.00 (circa 1925).
Current Value: $35.00-$50.00.

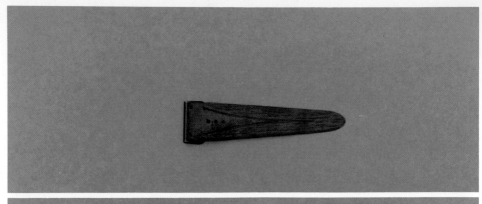

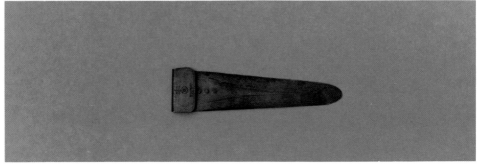

Combination bookmark and letter opener, 4″ long. Radial hammering and incised decorative linework. Late mark.
Original Price: .50 (circa 1925).
Current Value: $45.00-$60.00.

Chapter Twelve
Some Additional Prices

Over and above the many items pictured and priced in this book, there are several other Roycroft art metal objects deserving description and evaluation. These selected pieces are listed below for your information.

Bracelet, sterling silver with embossed floral design....$160.00-$190.00.

Cigar box, hammered-copper with applied medallion on the lid, 6" X 9"....$300.00-$350.00.

Chafing dish, ceramic dish with lid fits into an elaborate hammered-copper base with attached handles and riveted construction, overall height 8", basal diameter 14".......$750.00-$950.00.

Cigarette stand/ashtray, hammered-copper construction, 28½" high...$600.00-$800.00.

Hat pin, circular hammered-copper dome-form attached to the top of a long hat pin....$65.00-$90.00.

Picture frame, rectangular form, 6¾" X 9¼", hammered-copper with rippled edges......$160.00-$210.00.

Smoker's set, consisting of four pieces: humidor, cigarette cup, and ashtray/matchbox holder, with matching 6" X 13" rectangular tray.....$425.00-$500.00.

Vase, American Beauty type, long cylindrical neck with flared mouth and body, overall height 22", basal diameter 7¾"......$900.00-$1200.00+.

Vase, American Beauty, overall height 7".......$275.00-$350.00.

Vase, buttress type, 8" high, cylindrical body with four attached buttress forms, decorative nickel-silver squares applied below the lip.......$1100.00-$1300.00+.

Hand-Hammered Copper

Ink-Pot 513—Price, $4.50
Diameter 3 in., Height 3 in.
For Milady's writing desk

Flower-Bowl 235.   Price $6
A handsome recent design.
Height 5 in. Diameter 5 in.

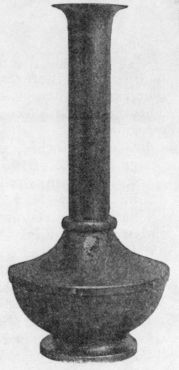

No. 211, 7 in., $5; 210, 12 in.,
$12; 201, 19 in., $18.

Diam. 11 in.   240 Flower-Bowl, $10.   Height 3 in.

Chapter Thirteen

Original Advertisements

The following selection of original Roycroft art metal advertisements were taken from such publications of the period as *The Philistine, Roycroft* and *The Roycrofter*, these dating from 1914 to 1930.

They have been included here in an effort to further illustrate the incredible variety of items that were made at the Roycroft Copper Shop, and to give additional perspective regarding the prices at which such items were sold.

A PAIR *of book ends with a sculptured leather panel of an old Viking boat—a desk lamp with real Vellum skin shade bound with rawhide—and a five-piece desk set chased and modeled in a modern motif make an ensemble for the desk that stimulates correspondence.*

920	Lamp with real Vellum shade, 15" high	$25.00
730	Desk Set, pad size 14" x 21"	22.00
364	Book End, Viking ship design, in sculptured leather panel	9.00

𝕿HE *unusual if coupled with artistic merit will compel attention and draw comment that is always gratifying to the hostess. These trindles and the Steuben bubbly glass vase in its handwrought holder is sure to bring forth this gratifying comment.*

433   Trindles, 8″ long, [pair] $12.00
248   Vase, 6¼″ high, with Steuben Bubbly Glass
     container 6.50

𝖂ITH *the needs of the smoking reader, or the reader and smoker in mind, this table group has been assembled. This handwrought lamp has a hexagonal real Vellum skin shade and the wise old owl in the sculptured leather panel of the book ends looks on approvingly.*

921   Lamp, 16″ high, with real Vellum shade $35.00
361   Book Ends, Owl design in sculptured leather
     panel 5.00
635   Tobacco Bowl, 5″ diameter 8.00
617   Pipe Knocker, 7″ diameter 4.00
655   Ash Bowl, with cigar rest, 3½″ diameter . . .   2.50

$\mathfrak{T}$HESE *pieces will suggest an idea for the furnish-*
ing of your writing table where a note of simplicity
is to be carried out. The flower holder with its bud or
blossom and the candles with their touch of color soften
the severity of line of the set.

729	Desk Set, pad size 14″ x 21″	$14.50
420	Candlesticks, 8″ high, [pair].	5.50
111	Vasette, 6″ high	1.60
427	Candlestick, 3¼″ diameter	3.00

$\mathfrak{T}$HIS *reading lamp is Colonial in its feeling and*
with the rawhide thong binding on the oval real
vellum skin shade makes one of our most successful lamps.
$\mathfrak{C}$ *The book ends with old brass frames and the quaint*
dutch figures in sculptured leather add a pleasing bit
of color. Add to these the ash bowl, cigarette box and
paper knife and you have a setting for a table that invites
you to "gather around" on the long winters' evening.

922	Lamp, 20″ high, oval shade of real vellum. . .	$45.00
365	Book Ends, "Hans" and "Gretchen" design in sculptured leather panels	10.00
658	Ash Bowl with cigar rest, 3½″ diameter	3.00
546	Paper Knife, 8″ long	1.00
625	Cigaret Box, cedar lined, holds 50 cigarets. .	11.00

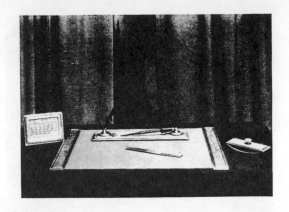

*D*IGNITY—*strength—restraint—such quality as you find in the big executive we have endeavored to work into the design and execution of these desk accessories that he will use. Such a token of appreciation to your chief either from the individual or the group would make a fitting vehicle for conveying your marks of loyalty and esteem.*

731 Desk Set, pad 19″x24″, Antique brass finish $67.50
     Etched silver finish......................   96.00
The Parker Fountain Pens are extra and may be
    purchased from us or through your stationer.

*T*HIS *group may suggest a serving table or buffet decoration and in turn the bowl and candlesticks may be used for the table center grouping and the tray is an ideal size for the cocktail or after-dinner coffee.*

431 Candlesticks, 5½″ long [pair]............. $6.00
250 Bowl, 6″ diameter......................   4.00
830 Tray, 19½″ long........................   8.00

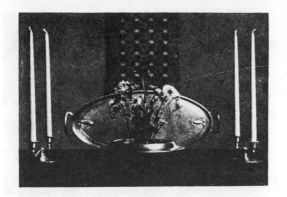

$\mathcal{T}$HE *problem of your dining table decoration is solved with the grouping suggested here. The two branch candle holder symbolize grace and dignity, the bowl lends itself to a variety of flower arrangements and the tray is of generous size and carries out the graceful lines of the candelabra.*

432	Two-Branch Candelabra, 7½″ long [pair] . . .	$12.50
240	Bowl, 11″ diameter	11.00
815	Tray, 22″ long	17.50

$\mathcal{T}$HIS *group suggest various uses to the hostess. The card trays with their hand chased and modeled designs are almost a necessity—the long tray for serving a cup of cold water to the thirsty guest makes the service a ceremony. The candlesticks either in pairs or sets of fours find their place either on the mantel, dining table or side board.*

428	Candlesticks, 3½″ high, [pair]	$6.50
825	Tray, 15″ long	5.50
1002A	Oval Card Tray, 7″ long	3.00
1000E	Round Card Tray, 6″ diameter	3.00
1007	Card Tray, 7″ diameter	6.50

FOR those who take their correspondence seriously this generous sized desk set—with lamp large enough to shed ample light over all will make a strong appeal. The book ends have sculptured leather panels with Comedy and Tragedy masque and the vase with bouquet of flowers may give you the inspiration you have sought for.

902	Lamp, 14″ high	$27.50
703	Desk Set, pad 16 x 24	21.00
362	Book Ends, Tragedy and Comedy Masque design in Sculptured leather panels	6.00
218	Vase, 5½″ high	5.00

IN these days when smoking knows no gender the demand for ash trays and cigarette holders is greater than ever. Also shown is a selection of book ends to hold the few choice volumes that you want within easy reach. For the gift occasion or for bridge prizes these will help solve the problem.

657	Ash Tray, with Glass Liner, 4¼″ diameter	$1.70
648	Cigaret Holder	2.00
651	Ash Tray, 4½″ square	2.00
644	Arm Chair Ash Tray, 2″ diameter, 15″ strop	2.80
653	Cigaret Holder and Tray, 4½″ square	4.00
354	Book Ends, 4″ high	2.20
356	Book Ends, 5″ high	5.00
353	Book Ends, 5″ high	4.00
355	Book Ends, 5″ high	4.00

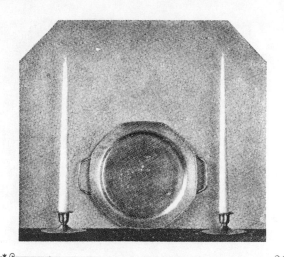

NOT only as a decorative feature for the dining room mantel, but used in pairs or better still in a set of four, these candlesticks with the long stately tapers add a distinctive and colorful note to the table. The tray is just the right size for a creamer and sugar or will hold a half dozen glasses for service during the evening.

426	Candlesticks, 4'' diameter [pair]	$4.50
826	Tray, 10'' diameter.....................	5.50

ROYCROFT Handwrought Copper bears the marks of the worker's hammer. It has the human touch and brings a reaction of brotherliness and friendliness to its owner.

531	Ink Pot, 3½'' diameter..................	$3.50
534	Pen Tray, 7'' long	2.50
543	Memo or Bridge Pad....................	3.00
535	Calendar 3½'' high	1.50
536	Roll Blotter, 4¾'' long.................	1.70
530	Slip-On Blotter Corners, 3'' x 3''.........	5.00
532	Stationery Holder, 3'' high..............	2.60

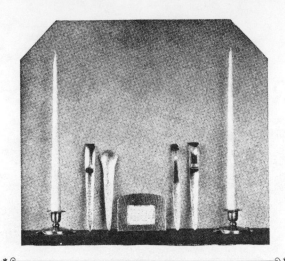

𝕬S souvenirs, bridge prizes, or remembrancers, Roy-croft paper knives, perpetual calendars and candlesticks give unusual satisfaction. They are so craftlike and unique.

424	Candlesticks, 3½'' diameter [pair]	$4.00
516	Paper Knife, 8'' long.	1.40
533	Paper Knife, 7¼'' long.	1.40
555	Calendar, 3¼'' high.	1.50
517	Paper Knife, 8'' long.	1.80
518	Paper Knife, 8'' long.	1.40

¶ The charm of candle lighting is heightened by the unusual effect produced by closely massed candles.

436	"The Big Six," illustrated above	$10.00
433	"The Trindle," illustrated page 3 . . . . .each	6.00
438	"The Straight Eight," with holder for eight candles	12.50

𝕽OYCROFT Handwrought Copper is in Aurora Brown and Old Brass. Every piece is the guaranteed product of skilled copper craftsmen and made to give full satisfaction. As gifts you can not present anything at equal cost that will be more acceptable than these Roycroft Handwrought Copper Objects of Art. We pay all shipping charges.

FOR GRADUATION GIFTS

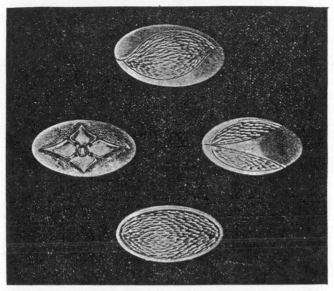

Left No. 2311   Bottom No. 2308   Top No. 2309   Right No. 2310

HANDMADE STERLING SILVER PINS & BRACELETS

The Roycrofters have used this expressive metal with rare judgment and understanding in the fashioning of these pins. They will give supreme satisfaction to both giver and user. Prices: Nos. 2308, 2309, and 2310 are priced at $3.50 each, and No. 2311 is $5.00

The Sterling Silver Bangle Bracelets are about one-eighth inch wide and are hand-hammered. They are usually worn in pairs. Sizes: small, 7 inches; medium, 7½ inches; large, 8 inches. Price $1.50 each, $3.00 a pair.

The Band Bracelets are beautifully fashioned by hand and modeled with a charming flower design. They have an opening on the under side which allows for them to be easily adjusted to any size wrist. Price $5.00

Roycroft Handwrought Copper

has a Permanent Decorative Value in the Scheme of Home Decoration and Office Furnishing

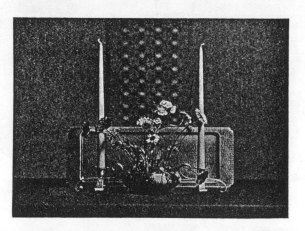

431   Candlesticks, 5½" long (pair) $6.00
250   Bowl, 6" diameter 4.00
830   Tray, 19½" long 8.00

729   Desk Set, pad size 14" x 21" $14.50
420   Candlesticks, 8" high, (pair) 5.50
111   Vasette, 6" high 1.60
427   Candlestick, 3¼" diameter 3.00

Roycroft Handmade Copper

645—Handwrought Copper Ash Tray with two cigar rests and jade glass liner, 5½" in diameter Price ----------------- $6.00

663—Three Bookish Copper Containers for cigarettes. Price------$10.00

372—Copper Bookends onlays on brass 5" high. Price $7.50
373—Copper Bookends onlays on nickel-silver, 5" high. Price ----------------- $9.00

250—Copper Bowl 6" in diameter. Price------ $4.00

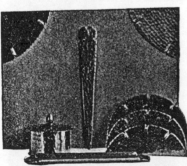

722—Desk Set of 5 pieces: Desk Pad, Stationery Holder, Ink Cup, Pen Tray, Paper Knife. Price ---------- $17.50

218—Copper Vase 5½" high. Price --- $5.00

THE ROYCROFTERS, EAST AURORA, N. Y.

ROYCROFT
SHEFFIELD
S I L V E R

(which is Sterling Silver over Copper)

FOR
WEDDING
GIFTS

Two-branch Candle-
sticks, 6 inches high
The Pair $26.25

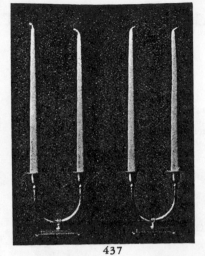

437

Straight-eight
Candelabra,
21 inches
long. Each $18.50

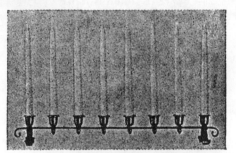

438

Cream and Sugar
Tray, 15 inches
long. Each . $8.00

825

THE ROYCROFTERS, EAST AURORA, N. Y.

Bibliography

Hamilton, Charles F., *Roycroft Collectibles*. New York: A.S. Barnes and Co., 1980.

Johnson, Bruce, *The Official Identification and Price Guide to Arts and Crafts*, New York: House of Collectibles, 1988.

Levulis, Stanley and Dorothy, *The Story of Elbert Hubbard and the Roycrofters of East Aurora*. New York: Stanley and Dorothy Levulis, 1971.

Ludwig, Coy L. *The Arts and Crafts Movement in New York State 1890s-1920s*. Layton, Utah: Peregrine Smith, 1983.

Shay, Felix, *Elbert Hubbard of East Aurora*. New York: Wm. H. Wise & Co., 1926.

Author's Note: All of the above books are highly recommended to those wishing to know more about Elbert Hubbard and Roycroft collectibles.